COUNTRY EXPLORERS

CHILE

Jennifer A. Miller

Lerner Publications Company • Minneapolis

Lerner Publications Company
A division of Lerner Publishing Group, Inc.
241 First Avenue North
Minneapolis, MN 55401 U.S.A.

Website address: www.lernerbooks.com

Library of Congress Cataloging-in-Publication Data

Miller, Jennifer A.
    Chile / by Jennifer A. Miller
        p.   cm. – (Country explorers)
        Includes index.
        ISBN–13: 978–0–7613–5319–5 (lib. bdg. : alk. Paper)
        1. Chile—Juvenile literature. I. Title.
    F3058.5.M55 2011
    983—dc22   2009031515

Manufactured in the United States of America
1 – VI – 7/15/10

Table of Contents

Welcome!

Let's travel to Chile! Chile is the longest and narrowest country in the world. On a map, it looks like a string bean.

Chile sits on the southern end of South America. Peru and Bolivia lie to the north. Chile's eastern neighbor is Argentina. The Pacific Ocean touches the west and south sides of Chile.

The Pacific Ocean meets the shore on Chile's long coast.

4

PERU

BOLIVIA

BRAZIL

PARAGUAY

ANDES MOUNTAINS

ATACAMA DESERT

OJOS DE SALADO

CHILE

Valparaiso

★ **Santiago**

LLAIMA VOLCANO

ACONCAGUA R.

BÍO-BÍO R.

CENTRAL VALLEY

ANDES MOUNTAINS

LAGO LLANQUIHUE

CHILOÉ ISLAND

PACIFIC OCEAN

URUGUAY

ARGENTINA

ATLANTIC OCEAN

TIERRA DEL FUEGO (ARGENTINA)

EASTER ISLAND

MILES
0   3

0   2.5
KILOMETERS

	mountain
	desert
	volcano
★	country's capital

MILES
0   200   400

0   200   400
KILOMETERS

Snow dusts the peaks of the Andes Mountains in southern Chile.

From Ocean to Mountain

Chile's land gets higher from the west to the east. High plains, or flat areas, lie just east of the coast. The steep Andes Mountains stand along the eastern border.

6

From north to south, the land changes wildly. In the north is the Atacama Desert. This northern desert can go years without getting rain. In Chile's center are lakes, rivers, and volcanoes. Southern Chile has thick forests. This area also has many islands.

Map Whiz Quiz

Take a look at the map on page 5. Trace the outline of Chile onto a sheet of paper. Can you find the Pacific Ocean? Mark this part of your map with a *W* for west. Next, find the country of Argentina. Mark it with an *E* for east. Pick out two colors. Color Argentina with one. Use the other for the water in and around Chile.

The Atacama Desert in northern Chile is the driest desert in the world.

Volcanoes

Chile lies on the Ring of Fire. This area includes the coasts of many countries that touch the Pacific Ocean. It is called the Ring of Fire for its many volcanoes and earthquakes. Chile has more than two thousand volcanoes. About fifty of them are active. This means they send out smoke and ash. Ojos del Salado in Chile is the world's tallest active volcano. It is 22,664 feet (6,908 meters) high.

Llaima Volcano in central Chile erupted in 2008.

Ojos del Salado is a big volcano in northern Chile.

Volcanoes can create disasters if they erupt, or blow up. But they can also be useful. They heat the water nearby. Chile uses the steam and heated water for energy.

The Chuquicamata copper mine is in the Atacama Desert. This mine has produced more copper than any other mine in the world.

Mining

Northern Chile has many mines. The mines hold big supplies of minerals. Chileans mine iron, copper, zinc, and even gold and silver. Chile leads the world in copper mining. Chile's copper is used to make coins and building materials. Some household goods are created from copper too.

Chuquicamata Copper Mine

Chuquicamata is the largest open-pit mine in the world. Miners work on top of the land, not in tunnels underground. The mine is 2.5 miles (4 kilometers) long, 1.3 miles (2 km) wide, and 2,100 feet (640 m) deep. Special trucks carry copper away from the mine. The trucks' tires are 11 feet (3.4 m) wide.

Chile used to mine a lot of a mineral called nitrate. Towns were built around these mines. But then the mines closed. And people moved out of the towns, creating ghost towns.

Nitrate miners built this town in northern Chile in the 1930s. It was abandoned in the 1990s.

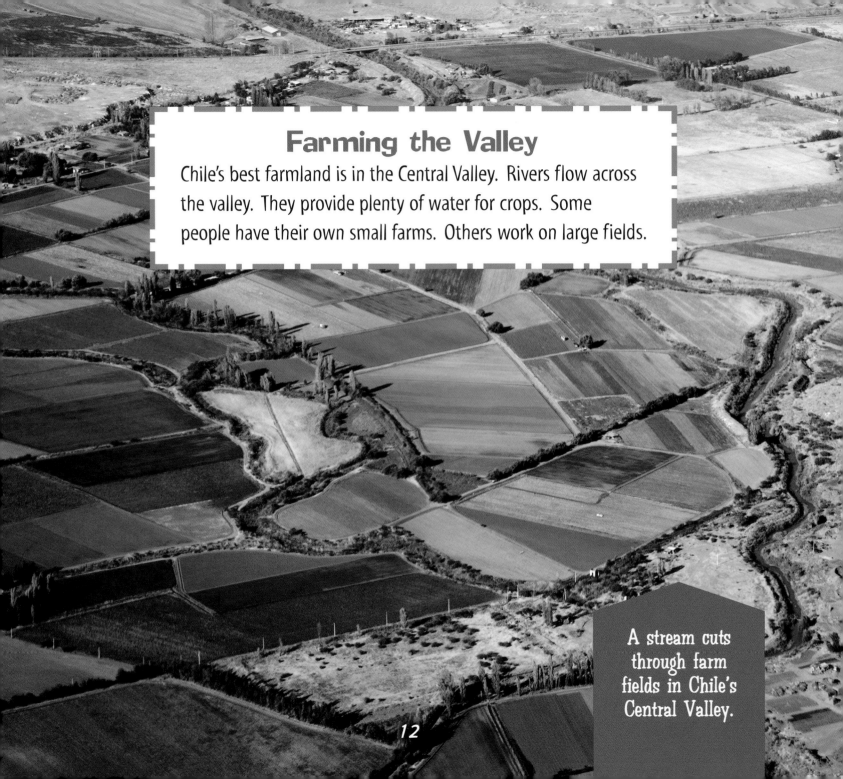

Farming the Valley

Chile's best farmland is in the Central Valley. Rivers flow across the valley. They provide plenty of water for crops. Some people have their own small farms. Others work on large fields.

A stream cuts through farm fields in Chile's Central Valley.

12

Many farmers grow wheat for a living. They also grow beans, potatoes, corn, and more. Lots of Chilean meals are made from these crops.

Season Switch

Chile is located south of the equator. The equator is an imaginary line around Earth. Seasons south of the equator are the opposite of seasons north of the equator. Most crops grow in Chile from December to March. Chile has warm weather during that time.

This farmer grows grapes on a farm in central Chile.

13

Food

Empanadas are Chile's national food. A meat filling is heaped onto a circle-shaped pastry. The dough is then folded over. Next, the edges are sealed.

These empanadas have a filling made of chicken and spices.

The cook then either bakes or fries the empanada. One popular filling is beef mixed with onions and seasonings.

A Chilean family enjoys lunch at an outdoor restaurant.

Back in Time

Long ago, Chile's native people were called Araucanians. They all spoke the same language. But three cultures lived in different areas. These cultures were the Picunche (people of the north), the Mapuche (people of the land), and the Huilliche (people of the south).

The people of these cultures hunted animals and grew crops. They raised animals such as llamas and alpacas.

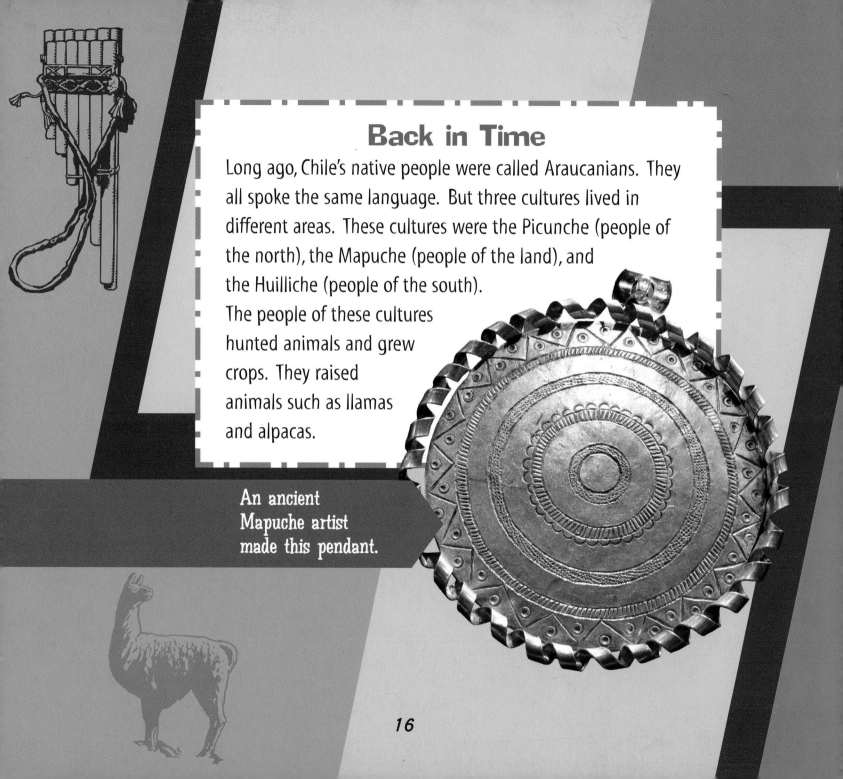

An ancient Mapuche artist made this pendant.

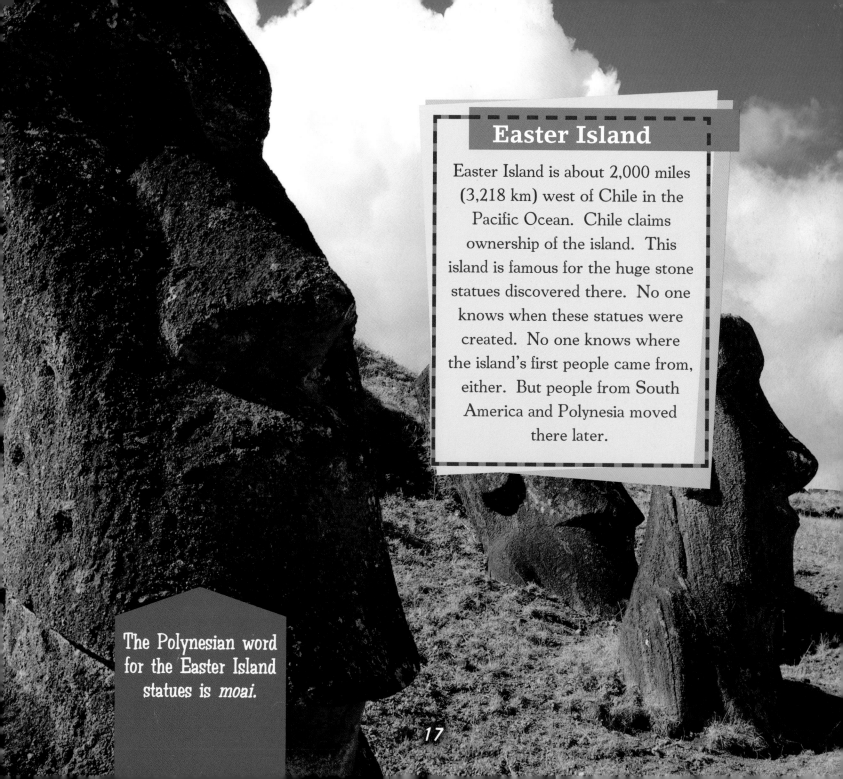

Easter Island

Easter Island is about 2,000 miles (3,218 km) west of Chile in the Pacific Ocean. Chile claims ownership of the island. This island is famous for the huge stone statues discovered there. No one knows when these statues were created. No one knows where the island's first people came from, either. But people from South America and Polynesia moved there later.

The Polynesian word for the Easter Island statues is *moai*.

Chilean People

About five hundred years ago, Spanish soldiers came to Chile. They met the native people who were living there. Many soldiers started families with the local people. Most Chileans are part native South American and part Spanish. They are called mestizos.

Chileans wait for a bus in the capital city of Santiago.

Mapuche people from northern Chile perform a traditional dance.

Ancient Art

Geoglyphs *(below)* are giant outdoor drawings. Ancient artists drew geoglyphs on the land. The art includes pictures of animals, people, and simple shapes.

Some native people still live in Chile. The Mapuche live in south central Chile. The northern mountains are home to the Aymara. And the Huilliche are down in the islands of southern Chile.

19

Speaking Spanish

Spanish is the official language
of Chile. Chileans speak very fast.
Other Spanish-speaking people
sometimes have a hard
time understanding Chileans.

Most Chilean magazines
and newspapers use the
Spanish language.

20

Family Words

Here are the Spanish words for family members.

grandfather	abuelo	(ah-BWAY-loh)
grandmother	abuela	(ah-BWAY-lah)
father	padre	(PAH-dray)
mother	madre	(MAH-dray)
uncle	tío	(TEE-oh)
aunt	tía	(TEE-ah)
son	hijo	(EE-hoh)
daughter	hija	(EE-hah)
brother	hermano	(ehr-MAH-noh)
sister	hermana	(ehr-MAH-nah)

A few native languages, such as Aymara and Mapuche, still exist. Many words that Chileans use are taken from the Mapuche language. Chile's name may even come from the Mapuche word *chilli*. This means "where the land ends."

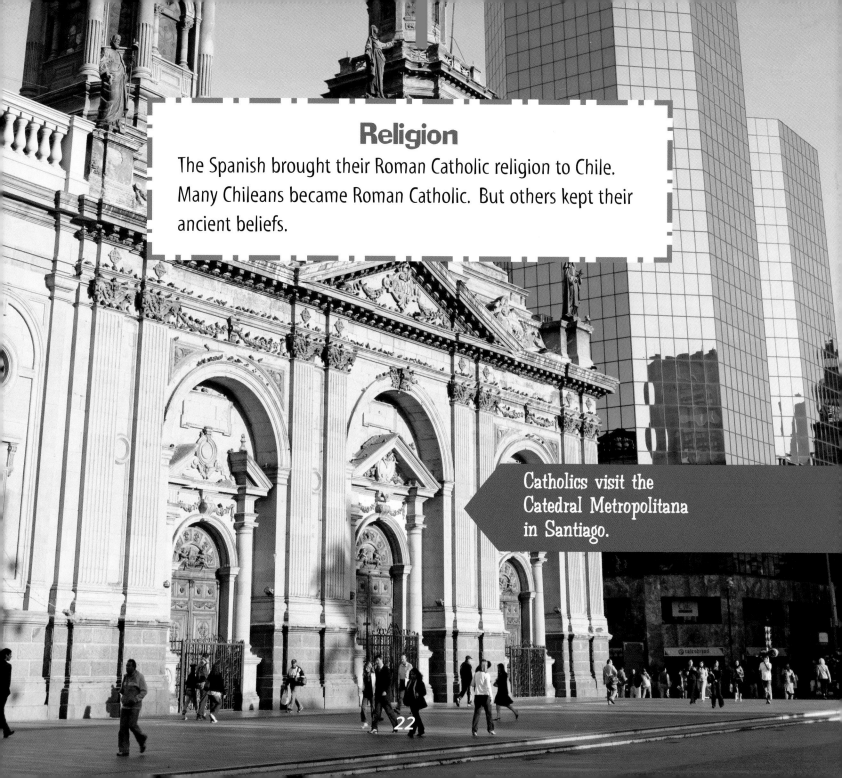

Religion

The Spanish brought their Roman Catholic religion to Chile. Many Chileans became Roman Catholic. But others kept their ancient beliefs.

Catholics visit the Catedral Metropolitana in Santiago.

22

The Mapuche believe in good and evil spirits. Shamans are people who try to speak with these spirits. Shamans believe magic can protect villages and heal people.

Mapuche shamans sing and play drums during a religious festival.

Holidays

Chile's Independence Day is on September 18. It marks the date in 1810 when Chile claimed independence from Spain.

A man sells handmade kites in Santiago for Chile's Independence Day.

This day also marks the beginning of spring. People dance and eat all night. Children fly kites in contests. And soldiers march in a parade.

Did You Know?

During Christmas, Santa Claus is very popular. December, when Christmas is celebrated, is hot in Chile. But many people wear Santa's heavy red suit despite the warm weather.

A Chilean cowboy marches in an Independence Day parade.

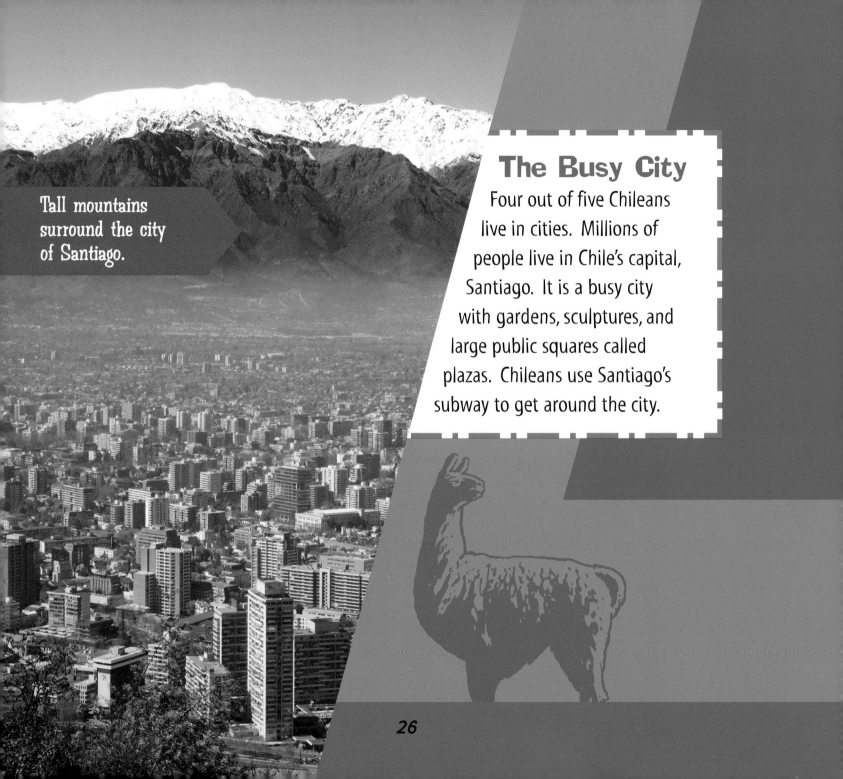

Tall mountains surround the city of Santiago.

The Busy City

Four out of five Chileans live in cities. Millions of people live in Chile's capital, Santiago. It is a busy city with gardens, sculptures, and large public squares called plazas. Chileans use Santiago's subway to get around the city.

Santiago is in the Central Valley of Chile.
So are Chile's major factories.

Chileans catch the
subway in Santiago.

Crowded Homes

People move to Santiago from all over Chile. But there are not enough jobs or places to live for everyone who comes. *Casetas* are homes for low-income families. Many of these homes are falling apart.

This family moved into a tent while waiting for space in a low-income apartment home.

Shacks line a city hillside on the edge of the Atacama Desert.

The poorest families live in crowded areas called *callampas,* which means "mushrooms." These areas are filled with small shacks. They seem to spring up quickly. Children in callampas often don't go to school or have enough to eat.

Family Life

Chilean families are close. Children live with their parents until they are married. Many children who live in the countryside work with their families. Boys may help take care of llamas and other animals. And girls often make scarves and caps to sell at the local market.

Families enjoy a picnic lunch in a park in Santiago.

30

Chileans use two last names. The first last name is the father's last name. The second is the mother's last name before she was married. In normal use, the mother's last name is dropped.

A father and his son use horses to bring vegetables to a farmer's market.

Schooling

Children must go to school for eight years. Then they may choose to continue after the age of fourteen. All students wear uniforms.

Every school has different colored uniforms. These children wear maroon and gray.

Chilean students study Spanish, math, science, and history. At recess, students usually play soccer, jump rope, or play *bolitas* (marbles).

This Chilean school band is ready to march in a parade.

Game Time

Soccer is called *fútbol* in Chile. It is the favorite pastime of many Chileans. Children play soccer after school. And whole families love to go to soccer games in stadiums.

Boys play in a soccer tournament on Easter Island.

34

Rodeo is Chile's national sport. It is popular in rural areas. In a Chilean rodeo, two riders work together to stop a calf from running. They wear large, flat-topped hats; boldly colored ponchos; and big, black boots.

Chilean cowboys are known as gauchos.

Outdoor Fun

Chileans have lots of different ways to spend time outdoors. A beach is never very far away. Many people enjoy swimming, fishing, and boating. And the mountains are a perfect place for hiking and skiing.

Visitors crowd a sunny beach near Valparaiso, Chile.

36

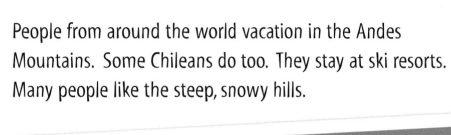

People from around the world vacation in the Andes Mountains. Some Chileans do too. They stay at ski resorts. Many people like the steep, snowy hills.

Skiers hit the slopes at a Chilean resort in the Andes Mountains.

Wildlife

Chile's animals are different in each part of the country. In the northern desert region, only a few animals can survive. One is the gray gull. The *pudú* lives in the southern forests. It is the smallest deer in the world. Penguins and sea lions make their home among the islands in the south.

Penguins come to Chile's southern coasts to lay eggs and raise babies.

The chinchilla is a small rodent originally from Chile. The chinchilla was hunted for its soft fur for hundreds of years. It is almost extinct.

Chinchillas live in northern Chile. They eat grass, seeds, and insects.

The Arts

Many famous writers are from Chile. Gabriela Mistral is a poet. In 1945, she was the first Latin American to win the Nobel Prize in Literature. Isabel Allende is known around the world for her stories.

Isabel Allende carries a copy of her 2009 book *La Isla Bajo el Mar (Island Beneath the Sea)*.

Music and dance are also important to Chileans. The panpipe is a traditional musical instrument used in folk music. The national dance is the *cueca*. It is danced at many festivals and holidays.

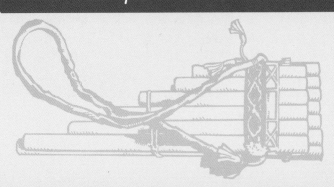

Chileans dance the cueca at a festival in the countryside.

41

Crafts

Chileans use local materials to make crafts. Northern Chileans make clothing and rugs from alpaca and llama hair. Atacama residents use cactus wood to make carvings and panpipes. The Mapuche people work with silver and a gem called lapis lazuli. They make jewelry and decorations.

A woman weaves cloth from alpaca hair in a village in central Chile.

Hola abuelo (Hi, grandpa)!

We took a boat today to Chiloé Island. We learned a Chiloé folktale about brujos. Brujos are wizards on the island. Every night, they take a ghost ship, Calueche, out into the ocean. They rescue the spirits of people who drowned.

I learned more stories and wrote them down in my journal. I'll tell you all about them when I come back.

See you soon!
Carmen

Grand__
Your
Anywh

Chiloé Island, Chile

43

THE FLAG OF CHILE

Chile's flag is white, blue, and red with a white star. The white stripe represents snow on the Andes Mountains. The white star is for progress and honor. The blue stands for the sky. And the red represents the blood shed for independence.

FAST FACTS

FULL COUNTRY NAME: Republic of Chile

AREA: 292,260 square miles (756,950 square kilometers), or a little bigger than Texas

MAIN LANDFORMS: the Andes mountain range; the Atacama Desert; the geyser El Tatio; the lake Lago Llanquihue; the islands Chiloé, Tierra del Fuego, and Easter

MAJOR RIVERS: Aconcagua, Bío-Bío

ANIMALS AND THEIR HABITATS: fox, frog, hare, lizard, mountain cat, puma, rhea, toad, weasel, wolf (forests); alpaca, Andean condor, flamingo, hummingbird, llama, Magellan conure (mountains); pelican, penguin, petrel (coast); coatis, goat, rabbit, rat, red hummingbird, seal (islands); congrio, crab, lobster, mussel, oyster, scallop, sole, swordfish (ocean)

CAPITAL CITY: Santiago

OFFICIAL LANGUAGE: Spanish

POPULATION: about 16,770,000

GLOSSARY

ancient: from a long time in the past

capital: a city where the government is located

continent: any one of seven large areas of land. The continents are Africa, Antarctica, Asia, Australia, Europe, North American, and South America.

culture: the way of life, ideas, and customs of a particular group of people

desert: a dry, sandy region

map: a drawing or chart of all or part of Earth or the sky

mountain: a part of Earth's surface that rises high into the sky

plain: a large area of flat land

plateau: a large area of high, level land

religion: a system of belief and worship

shaman: a person believed to talk with spirits and use magic to treat the sick

slum: an area of a city where low-income citizens live

traditional: something that people in a particular culture pass on to one another

volcano: an opening in Earth's surface through which hot, melted rock shoots up. Volcano can also refer to the hill or mountain of ash and rock that builds up around the opening.

TO LEARN MORE

BOOKS

Holiday, Jane. *Exploring Chile with the Five Themes of Geography.* New York: PowerKids Press, 2005. Chile's geography, including desert areas, plains, volcanoes, and rain forests, is presented.

Kwek, Karen. *Welcome to Chile.* Milwaukee: Gareth Stevens, 2004. Learn more about Chile's religion, people, food, arts, sports, and history.

WEBSITES

Easter Island: Land of Giant Stones and Mysteries
http://www.socialstudiesforkids.com/articles/geography/easterisland1.htm
This site shares some fun facts and asks some interesting questions about the mysterious Easter Island.

Geographia: Chile
http://www.geographia.com/chile
Read about Chile's beautiful land, history and culture, and the islands.

Time for Kids: Around the World: Chile
http://www.timeforkids.com/TFK/teachers/aw/wr/main/0,28132,1113147,00.html
This fun site includes a sightseeing guide and some common lingo.

INDEX